I0004607

The Zealots Guide

To Computer Security
2013-14

By Brian Taylor

Introduction

Information security management while primarily focusing upon the inherent risks in the "weaknesses" within a system, are beginning in many ways to now extend their collective glances outward.

While at that first glance, some of the incredible leaps forward in both defensive and offensive security practices look slight to the untrained eye, the security world is both nervous and intrigued by these innovations.

Managing intervention where the risk was concerned, had been the battle cry of the last generation of introverted tech savvy business. They begged for stronger fences against the ever growing threats of; information theft, penetration exploits, and degrading attacks of online vandalism. In many cases the unprovoked exploitations of inherent tech weaknesses, through ddos. attacks, and database architecture information (now widely available,) was unavoidable.

As we move into the era of mobile operating systems in their fourth generations and higher evolutions, with their advantages against detection. One thing became very clear to companies in 2012. The age of plausible deniability from security experts was no longer an excuse for the loss of resources.

Information was the great casualty of the ignorance that proceeded this era. Linux architecture rose above the simple "open source software" that nobody worried much about in the years that proceeded. Now with distributions of software that could mobilize attacks almost without a trace people had cause for concern.

Corporations lost billions of dollars to corporate level attacks, governments lost information vital to the safety of their military and intelligence communities.

Private citizens were still relying on freeware to protect their information.

Chapter 1. Treasonous Architecture

Little more than an inherent weakness in the fiber of our thinking would lead us in to the information age with technology that we didn't know could do a dangerous thing in the hands of children. ~ Brian Taylor

Let me begin by stating I am just the messenger. I have seen the capabilities of the little known operating systems and the better known operating systems in tutorials, in testing over private networks, and in result as reported by the media. I personally am not a writer of codes, exploits, malware, malicious code, or even the transferring of documents that have such materials within them.

However, to be a threat many now know that to tear down your website they don't need to log in, decrypt your 13 letter, number and special character password, and know your mothers maiden name.

They just need to know a handful of things that they can either learn from the tutorials that come packaged with a database install manual, or better still, watch how to ruin your entire website operation on any of the countless websites that teach exactly how to do just that.

They don't even need a computer anymore, They have a few older friends, a smart phone and might be 13 years old. But after watching a few videos, they need to see if what they read was true... Did you really leave your system running on an outdated server with no firewall?

They downloaded a file transfer app and tried a few times to brute force their way in and your security team saw them and said, "Happens all the time."

May 21 Austrian Police seize person and property on a 15 year old boy.

"Free Topiary" Was no longer a term to take lightly to some, The 18 year old in the UK had as many supporters who had no idea who or what he was but to security analysts he was the sign of the trend.

"Not only are the hackers getting younger they are multiplying and using systems which seem almost designed to avoid us."

Could be heard echoing through the halls of corporate America as the currency became threatened and investors as well as analysts were now marveling at the news on their new android phones.

To be fair, Linux and Android are not responsible for the proliferation of malicious and exploitative technology, they are simply the easiest way to implement the changes that are needed to make most security practices obsolete.

Linux to a purist is an marvelous thing, a technological triumph against the commercial stranglehold that has been imposed by the monopolization of the software industries since the earliest days of computing.

The Unix shell, and its many open systems allowed companies like Silicon Graphics do things with technology that computers produced for the home user wouldn't dare to catch up to until the mid 1990's.

Linux was a stab at creating rival architecture primarily to avoid cost of implementation. It was more than a clone, it was the hope of the designer that keeping software open and free to the public would necessitate positive growth and change for the better.

The implementation of freeware was the beginning for the community of professional coders and developers who would make such drastic shifts in the way software interacted, that only the coders knew what they were building and out of what.

The first exploits of software came from finding weaknesses, emulation coding made it possible to build the first programs that used these exploits.

It wasn't long until the companies that could make their stand against such software had a market.

As for Linux, it pioneered shifts into mixed software that permitted and even made possible some of the most fundamental advancements in integrated technology.

The license made it possible to shift code and profit so it became practical to be able to get into a network with different computer architectures, and the results were the beginnings of telnet, ssh, and the host of port packet sniffing technologies that still largely go by data authentication to allow or reject an incoming packet.

The packet... A simple bit of suggestive code that says, "Hello port, I am here to do this thing that you are designed to let me do, let me pass so we can get this done in a fraction of the time it took for the keystroke to make the letters of this sentence appear on the screen."

Ports allow the incoming information by if they look innocent, like a bouncer at a club it isn't his job to say, "How do I know you won't go straight into the bathroom and let in your underage girlfriend."

A packet is innocent, it might say "Transfer me to the caching system so this user is recognized by the website."

Or it might say, "I need to make a shift in a registry code that begins a process and the ten thousand guys behind me will add to that effect."

The port bouncer will seldom say to an innocent looking packet, "Get out of here you look shifty."

But even if he could he often can't get a chance, the staggering trend towards updating only segments of the security in a system make it easier in many cases to avoid the company computer and go straight to the next link in the chain.

The network of today runs through a VPN, a Virtual Private Network, with one tough computer in the front to make critical monitoring decisions and ten or a thousand computers behind it making ignorant ones.

The logic is sound until you look at outbound traffic. The packets exchanged by the most up to date systems out there won't be on the internet because they see it as a hazard.

Yet the money in exchange in the world is moving constantly through systems that, all day every day, are vulnerable to exploits at every "stop" along the way as the same kinds of algorithm technology that used to scan for viruses now scan for traces of encryption tech associated with money transfers.

And some of these programs are on the smart phones of the employee you just promoted to head of security. That isn't the nightmare he likes his job and you aren't his enemy.

Your competitor however has a guy just like him who's job it is to know who you just spent money on. Whether to improve relations with that legal firm, the tax people you are using, the corporate account rosters (and what you look like in the third quarter on facebook) as you just drove by in that new BMW and he raised an eyebrow and waved.

He might know more about you than your family does. You can bet its because every weakness in your brand new blade server system that shreds information across 4 continents at lightning speed like its nothing has an inherent operating system flaw or 23000 and they have that whole list.

They bought it on an auction site and have no compunction about using it because they know what you don't. You are using 2010 operating systems and there were so many updates you figured "Why upgrade?"

• Enumeration

Method: Some little bit of code is either accepted or thrown and if it happens a certain way you are screwed. Network enumeration, analysis and exploitation is about discovering the weaknesses that exist to plan a course of attack and making a stalwart effort to compromise a network based on such an analysis.

Understanding a network is a process like laying a map. To get anywhere, you need to know where you are going. So most of the research is done through analyzing the architecture itself of your system.

This can be done on a mobile system from your free wifi by the way.

Most of the information is gathered as legally as looking up a name in a phone book. Your ip is most likely static and your webpage that is uploaded from the same system as the corporate nightly audit is the first and most obvious target.

Not only that but your host computers all have names that identify them to an attacker usually, from the firewall name to the mail server you laid out a path that offers resistance sure, but these guys are cross training.

Line one of defense, the DNS should be a third party ISP (Write that down or highlight it)

Next you will be facing Ping Sweeps because they want to know what is "live" and what is sleeping. This used to be IMCP but the TCP is back in style and the echoes say more about your system than you really want anyone to know about. (If you have a third party DNS your phone will be ringing by now.)

There are ways to keep it under the radar though, as randomizing these pings can avoid detection sometimes thanks to software that actually does it for them, even from a modified phone.

As they literally trace the route of these signals they see where the door is, but worse they see the wide open network gaps that were long forgotten for whatever reason so a good policy is "One route to the web."

- Tunneling

Port forwarding, Remember your bouncer? This is the transmitting of data within private networks through public networks through a system of nodes.

This usually allows the private network to use the internet and is often also reverse utilized to walk in the back door and browse through the system for sensitive information. PPTP (point to point tunneling protocol) is the standard, the VPN (Virtual Private Network) is what makes it "reasonably safe."

The irony is many companies select at this stage to forgo encryption technology on a wink and a handshake along with some bravado about "Nobody getting past it."

Even a successful "clickjacking" on a social media account can get someone past your VPN. Its entirely possible to set up code to grab your information at the gate but its easier to get you to click a link to a picture of some sort.

Tools to prevent these attacks are simple enough to acquire you are looking for the following.

Means of mitigating the outgoing traffic to known and trusted domains. means of limiting your open ports. means of limiting ssh availability to the outside of your network. A means of controlling tcp transfers.

Mfs – Enterprise ™ has a few useful solutions as do other companies that specialize in these kinds of network control programs so make this part of your checklist.

- Bruteforce

Sounds like a crowbar right? Trial and error data decryption used by applications to decode your very precious password through a process that may or may not use tables to minimize the efforts and automate the process.

Infallible but quite possible to make ever more difficult by seeding the passwords. (Google it)

Blocking against brute force can be a simple enough implementation of limits on login attempts, ip bans after several failed attempts, analysis of suspicious login attempts through surveillance of the log.

Confirming these attempts should result in reporting the user, as well as implementing a solution. (Try APF Firewalls with BruteForce Detection by rfxnetworks ™)

• Spoofing

Creating an artificial packet or query string from your ip to make it look like it came from your own computer. Routers have thus far used destination IP to forward but ignore the source IP as that is only used for detection at the destination IP.

Prevention is often based on authentication between machines on a network, using an access control list to deny private IP on the downstream interface, Filtering of inbound and outbound traffic, configuring routers and switches, and enabling encryption sessions so that only trusted hosts can securely communicate with you.

Wireshark can if properly implemented prevent these attacks with some success, however you still want a filtering router that restricts the input to the input filter by not permitting a packet with the sources address that originates in an internal network.

Also filter the outgoing packets that have a different source address from the internal network to prevent attacks originating from the local site.

This can cut down drastically on denial of service attacks.

- Passwords

Seeding, creating a hash that identifies the password and converts the output to recognizable code so that the system acts as a lock.

Opie, Unix term for one time passwords (difficult to implement but worth it.)

Password systems that act in two parts can be devised to great success, if a login usb is required to sign in so much the better.

- Wireless

The router that is conquered becomes the enemy cannon... If they own the IP and they upload hacked firmware they can control your data.

Between scanning drones, attack scripts, many threats can be loaded onto your own router so if you suspect attack, start the hunt there as well.

Access points are easy to install so many of your workers might have set them up but not many of them were capable of setting proper protections.

Along come the attacks like "Wardriving" "Man In The Middle" "Plain Text Attacks" "Packet Sniffing" "Jamming" "NetJacking" "DDOS" and "Flooding" Most of these we could write whole chapters about, but whether they are passive or active they are attacks that rely on specific constants.

Keep your software and hardware drivers up to date, change the default SSID, Use WEP 128 with Mac filtering, and either disable the SSID broadcast or at the very least do not use a DHCP server to assign IP to clients on your network.

Rotate your static WEP regularly and actually set the router inside towards the center of the building and test outside for weaknesses, if your wifi can be reached from the parking lot set up a camera with accurate clocks to help trace an attack to its logical source.

- Discovery

New Exploits; are the weapon of choice for the tech developing hacker. I rather expect the news will stop announcing every potentially fatal flaw in your system after you recognize the trend is to hit targets after the bug fix. The common misconception is that every security patch that comes out fixes "most of the problems."

The truth is that these exploits lay dormant for ages and often its long after the hackers are done using them that you get the memo.

- Web Applications Flash, Injection of code, malicious browser script, stream injection (man in the middle attacks) Arbitrary code execution, cookie theft, false web pages.

WASC Dynamic Checking Compilers have shown significant promise in preventing injections by adding checks to the application.

This is primarily effective against sql and script injection.

- Forensics

The black hole effect is becoming more popular as the go to means of getting a ton of information quickly, utilizing a malicious script that executes machine code your browser literally regurgitates information to be sorted and processed (Often in a clone browser just to make sorting easier)

Just the tip of the ice burg as graphs can be made digitally to map vulnerabilities using countless methods.

There are theoretical solutions but currently they are a significant risk to the security in a network particularly an ad hoc network. It might be possible to use rerouting software during the post attack phase and often a malicious code remover can fix the problem.

Ideally heuristics can detect and prevent a black hole attack however if it is a cooperative one there is more danger, packet randomizers might be a solution if security isn't completely compromised.

• Fuzzers

Fuzzing a target is a way to find loopholes in security by using random data, "fault injection" used by many ethical hackers to safely determine what weaknesses exist in a system as well.

Ideally using a similar approach will show you the vulnerabilities they are looking for and make it possible to correct the vulnerabilities before they are found.

You had best be offline and have the correct authority before fuzzing your own systems as in many cases this will trigger most of your antivirus protocols.

• Bluetooth

Between bugging and phone exploiting they are not as safe as you think. There is a growing cause for alarm as more file sharing goes mobile that the trend will increase in data transfer through the devices but for now bugging is the worst of it.

You are probably fine as long as the device remains set to non-discoverable.

- Sniffers

Not quite what it sounds like a sniffer can be an analyzer for: packets, protocols, software, hardware, & even supposedly techniques.

Segmenting a larger network into smaller ones with bridges and routers and restricting communication with outside networks is the beginning of building a safer topology.

So keep your sensitive information offline as much as possible by using single point access through one machine that can be readily switched off on the offline side to communicate with the network ad hoc.

Or just use a lan cable during and disconnect it after. (saved a few bucks right there!)

- VOIP

Its the IP part that should stand out, voice over internet protocol is vulnerable to any or all of the packet transfer dangers in a system. Implementation in an unsecured environment is like an invitation. Worms, & Viruses have actually been the primary attacks on these systems so far but the trend will change quickly with new companies taking control of old VOIP software.

There are appliances that claim to defeat VOIP attacks but primarily as this battle rages on the most common attacks using VOIP remain in the form of Billing attacks, and DDOS.

- Debuggers

VDB Virtual Debugger, mostly for exploit analysis these script running table shifting, data gathering miniature tanks have been long overlooked by the novice hackers but as time goes by the usefulness is becoming well known so be ready to disable databases when there is a chance of these kinds of "attached foreign databases."

This is why private servers have a host panel under watch, when new folders are added, and when new databases appear, be aware of it happening.

- Penetration

Testing a system or defeating it in layers, that are considered outer and inner walls of defense while gathering information as they go the modern hacker is more intent on stealing something they already know is there. So penetration becomes less difficult as time goes by and data collection techniques advance.

It can be worth hiring a pen tester if you have a system that relies heavily on internet traffic. Be sure they can implement security improvements or you will have 10 pages of information that keeps you up at night and no solutions.

- RFID

Improperly formatted tagged cards that can be used a number of ways, between smart phone hacks through injection, and literal pass key cards the exploit-ability of the tech almost warrants its avoidance.

Unfortunately most bank cards come equipped now with RFID so it's not going away any time soon.

- It seemed prudent to give you this overview and while it seems daunting you might want to be familiar with all of these techniques long before we begin talking about securing your network, systems, email, vpns, etc.

Setting up a good defense is perhaps easier than you might expect seeing as we are now in a "Linux friendly era" we might just as well get used to the idea of implementing it whenever and wherever possible if you are the one in charge of deployment.

Linux based servers, Linux based Operating systems, Linux based Routers if you can get them, and you are way ahead of the curve defensively due to the nature of the system's architecture that in many cases is resistant or even impervious to viruses, malware, password cracking, and several other typical low level exploits...

However that is merely step one and only helpful for those of you deploying a new system. Even then we are still bound to the process of building a great defensive system employing a VPN, Firewall, User pass code system with permission limits, encrypted index if possible and a host of other systematic exploit prevention measures.

If you are using a Windows based system, there are more steps to take to make your system safe. Likewise some of the Oracle systems need proper measures and yes even Mac needs a good security perimeter. If you are on a Unix system you most likely have ten manuals covering security and likely won't gain as much from this book.

However I would say skim it for the online interface segments because many Linux users know Unix just well enough to create small problems for you, and will do so through command shell interface on any unsecured port access.

Before we dive in to the guts of things lets talk about cloud systems and security. We have a basic belief that cloud systems are risky for keeping sensitive information in, this is partially true so when using cloud servers its a good idea to work hard at keeping information broken up into less sensitive pieces.

Take online transaction records... Using an encrypted index you could logically keep customers records in 3 separate places as a measure of safety. One piece might be kept on a hard drive, One in a cloud, and one on paper perhaps.

A proper auditing software can be employed to assemble the information on an offline computer for analysis and billing.

It is prudent to think this way when you are trying to keep information secure.

Most cloud systems rely heavily on large server resources so its idealistic but logical to think that they are mostly secure.

They (cloud systems) are but for the people who make tidy lists of important things and archive them in clouds, there is no easier target in a breached system than a database full of organized lists.

Passwords are becoming a thing of the past as we witness more and more password leaks from massive corporations. Likewise we can't ignore the 88% increase in DDOS attacks in 2013 makes it the odds on favorite for your major threat assessments in the coming years.

So how do we prevent ourselves from being easily crippled by a DDOS?

First step is get your name servers out of the equation, use a CDN or

"Content Delivery Network" and deploy everything you can get away with to minimize your "Bullseye Factor." Use a hosting company that can rollback your website to prior to an attack at a moments notice.

A Bullseye factor is that mysterious factor that prompts an attack due to a company making claims or even statements that give people some excuse to hate said company.

That might sound crazy but a company image has plenty to do with who dislikes and attacks a corporation.

Even relatively well liked companies might develop a bullseye factor by angering the wrong group strategically by making a grandiose attention grabbing statement about national pride, or supporting law enforcement.

These are actually legitimate examples of what develops a bullseye factor. Other examples might include becoming notorious for endorsing a particular software or even simply perpetuating a bad customer service policy.

Ultimately most companies have no idea what prompted the malicious hacker but it could be anything from an NRA endorsement to a "Ban guns" statement, proving that; "Either side of any coin," will likely provoke fallout from the public somewhere.

Even the most harmless company might become victim of repeated attacks simply by denying spammers access to their forums.

My position on spammers is "Block them but outwit them." because even the mildest form of spam is likely dangerous for your customer and for your reputation as a business.

Discouraging spam is a simple matter if you have a web presence. Use a forum moderator, do not allow linking of any kind especially in comments. (Even non allowed comments can contain linking that might be malicious.)

If your forum is a community be certain to get every scrap of information possible before allowing any content on your site as most likely you will be the one liable for any damages done to the users of your site.

The same logic applies to email, do not open attachments if you did not solicit them personally and if possible not at all. Links in email are equally subject to being malicious and whenever possible use an analyzer to see if the links are indeed malicious.

We will go over spoofing a company address due to the recent influx of this kind of attack.

Unfortunately it is a simple thing to do, open an offline email handler like Thunderbird ™ or Outlook ™ create an account with a fictional company name or sadly a legitimate one and send out countless emails with spam links or worse.

When it happens you will feel helpless because nobody seems to know what to do about this situation.

"Get a copy of one of the emails for analysis and find its originating ip, and more importantly the isp and report it that way."

This can be done in most email programs by right clicking the email and viewing the source code. Take the numbers and search them in google and you will find countless ip look ups and even isp trackers to make life a bit easier.

Send the isp a record of the falsified data and if possible do it on legal letterhead. (They take that seriously)

A prudent and current list of Linux Systems to consider.
For Security:
- **Backbox** Linux providing ethical hacking tools
- **Caine** Providing investigative tools
- **Kali Linux** (replacing Backtrack 5)
- **NST** For Network Security Tools
- **Pentoo** A Gentu based pen testing tool suite
- Helix A Ubuntu based system with hardware and forensics built in to make security simpler.
- **Deft** A similar operating system focusing on detection and incident response

For Desktop Operating Systems based on networking needs.

- Small businesses might do well to use the **Xubuntu** operating system due to its speed, ease of use, user friendly interface, and restrictive permissions. Easy to install, network, and versatile enough for most of your needs.
- Mid Range businesses might do better with **Debian**, **Fedora**, **Ubuntu** or perhaps **Linux Mint**, due primarily to the versatility across the platforms and ease of use with servers often installed quickly and with minimal fuss.
- Large businesses should look at **Enterprise**, **Mepis**, **Fusion**, or in networks exceeding 25-30 computers per network combinations of tool specific distributions that focus on the tasks required.

With over 100 out of the box operating systems most of which: run beautifully, are either free or exceedingly low cost to implement, and are part of well maintained communities of developers, Linux is the first stop for building a secure work environment online.

There are other solutions that bear considering.

Other business based operating systems, Oracle ™ has some very compelling options.

Ultimately Windows ™ and Mac ™ users will be more likely to continue to use those operating systems however it will not be long before we see more Linux in business and at home due to the fast moving development of mobile operating systems that depend heavily on Linux Architecture.

Virtualization using Oracle systems on Windows Machines can be a great way to test or even deploy some systems providing you have a high resource computer to begin with.

Oracle has tutorials on this process and ISO files for many operating systems can be found online.

Generally once you download Virtual Box by Oracle you can create a virtual machine by having an ISO of the operating system you wish to implement/test by running Virtual Box and then sharing files with it through guest add ons.

The only part that you might find confusing is selecting the VDI (That is where you select the ISO) once you have done so and clicked start you will go through a legitimate installation of the operating system in the virtual environment.

Use a tutorial because each operating system has different space requirements.

(Or do as I did and just try it a few times until you figure it out.)

Meanwhile a virtual system when correctly implemented can be every bit as powerful as a committed system and far more portable between machines as they can be exported, cloned, transferred, and even modified. They can behave just like a regular operating system in most respects.

However there can be limitations based on configurations with certain systems particularly if you don't add and configure driver access etc.

Virtual servers can be far more practical than impractical but only when you configure them to behave like a host operating system so figure out what kind of time constraints you are working with before trying to make a weekend of a virtual cloud deployment.

Or just hire someone to do that part. (Far far easier)

Working with Linux can feel different at first, you will need cheat sheets for using the CLI if you have to make many modifications. It gets easier with practice and you can usually install a synaptic package manager with a simple command.

Generally something like: sudo apt-get synaptic package manager

Bash code is easy to find and therefore Linux is far more versatile to work with through a CLI "for a newcomer" than Windows was, Though the premise is the same. We only have a GUI or Graphical User Interface, to make it simpler and more appealing than using the CLI or Command Line Interface.

They do the exact same things, and with Linux we get an in between tool in the synaptic manager that accesses the repositories of code for programs that are ready to install "for free!"

For example if you need a Photo editing software and don't want to pay for a commercial product the open source alternatives already exist in the Linux repositories.

Gimp is arguably the same or similar enough that Photoshop in truth offered me as a consumer no viable reason to pay the upcharge for the branding.

As for selecting a Linux Distribution there are many deciding factors that should come in to play. If you are going to be networking many systems together several architectures that work together nicely will be a critical factor in your decision. It is important to note that to date the grand majority of Linux distributions work together will very little fuss due to the natural compatibility of their design.

In many cases there are libraries of additional software that work quite well with virtually any distribution of Linux. A Cent OS system can be working cohesively with a Debian system, being monitored by a secure Backbox System, and still operated via remote from anything from an Xubuntu system down the chain or up it in development terms.

What that means is that it is entirely possible to network together a completely unique network architecture with very little cost of implementation and honestly just a little know how.

Don't worry if you personally don't already know how. Learning these systems is not as difficult as you might think, in fact we could realistically give you an hour long tutorial and you might never need any tech support again.

You would invariably made one of a handful of operating system errors that are so common that I still make them myself on occasion. Then fixing them is something that takes minutes instead of days.

But lets take a look at the standard architecture of a business network and see if we can spot a suitable arrangement for you to try to implement as an example.

Starting from the Internet and working backwards we have the router with firewall and rules, then the gateway server, (Web server,) a series of PCs networked either in a Lan, or a Wireless Lan configuration. Additionally we might have networked in a Register of some kind or a library file server particularly if all of the machines are accountable for the same inventory.

This equals a private network and often employs a VPN system like Cisco. Most of the time this is the configuration whether there is ten computers or ten thousand where there is some variation of this configuration and it acts as "security through the gate."

Now we add in a mail server...

Suddenly between the gate and each individual PC we have sealed packets again (possibly) and this represents security breach 1

Voip for video conferencing, breach 2

Website integrated to the office, breach 3

Corporate server for audit, breach 4

We are just getting warmed up. Now if we change a few practices we can dramatically change the topography and make this far more secure.

Starting with the Router, this needs to be expensive? No this needs reinforcement from the firewall. Firewalls need to be intelligent about incoming and outgoing packets to avoid breaches.

Gateway Server, Does this act as a buffer where port forwarding is concerned or are we vulnerable to VOIP related exploits?

An easy solution is to have designated computers for VOIP off of the network and running through the router with only personal firewalls. No secure information should be on these machines so make them run incompatible software. (Windows 7 works great here)

Mail servers should be able to deliver mail internally using 128 bit encryption and external mail should be handled through different browsers to avoid corruption. (Mozilla for email from home on gmail)

For internal mail use an internal mail program no exceptions.

Another useful thing to have where running a website is concerned is a separate computer for administrating the website (Forums etc) and a designated computer for securely handling anything money related where the website is concerned. If possible run them on different operating systems, and use them *only for the website & with the browsers they use to interact with said website.*

If they browse elsewhere do so through separate accounts on those machines and through different browsers if possible. This creates an illusion of separate handling particularly if only the system admins can access the data that needs to be secure.

Corporate server data reporting should be done without the ugly obvious nature of every document being logical, have categories by pages and send as little information as you can get away with.

If you need to report daily revenue, inventory, and similar information do so through a logical code. $1500.00 could be AEKK if both parties know page 1 is for revenue and certain letters mean certain numbers.

If that was to much then at least don't spell out what the information is by saying "Revenue, 3/16/2014 $1500.00 depositing at 3:00 am in Citibank through account number agfwegf" <--- Obviously not a routing number.

It could be conveyed as simply as R1500CB3ARNS Which is Revenue $1500 Citibank 3AM Routing Number Standard.

Would your employees even know what it meant? How would anyone if you got creative you could put the info in plain sight. (Not that you should.)

Architecture plays a role in security but its a logical role. Linux offers us control over; what an employee can access, how they can use a system, and most importantly who was logged in when "X" happened.

That is a large part of the internal security suddenly seemingly "managed" but even then we have techniques that cost us by our ignorance.

Screen shots, Cellphone Cameras, (These are costly enough to warrant removal from the office workplace where employees are working with sensitive information.)

More importantly we want to know where our information goes and who is responsible for it. Your day to day account manager needs to be somewhat "less social" than your website admin who needs to be far "more social" than the online accounts manager and yes those should be people who don't mingle.

You don't want potential breaches between someone who knows how much money is sitting in pay pal and someone who is communicating with people in forums online.

Likewise you don't want the day to day account manager flirting with doing the social media for the company those positions just don't mix.

Office computers that need online access should have very little sensitive information on them. Information should be exposed to very little risk by use of external hard drives, Database Encryption, and finally interfaces that require only the most trusted personnel to access that information and only in a transparent way.

If the information about clients contains bank information see that it is kept in 3 parts, a numbered list of names, a numbered list of addresses, a numbered list of account info.

Guess which part needs to be secured?

A master system computer that can not in any way be online should be employed for the keeping of sensitive information. To process data over to that computer should be simple enough, whoever is responsible for the security should bring the data over hourly & should be who enters that data so that only one person is responsible for any of that information.

By now you want to strangle me for not just giving you exact directions. I know how you feel because I like easy answers but the easiest answer is to understand the methodology and find the software that best suits your company.

The easiest instructions I can give begin like this.

1. Evaluate the topography of your network or network needs to pinpoint your information systems in relation to the internet.
2. Create an ideal topography where the systems that seem the most crucial are disconnected or only minimally connected to the network.
3. Isolate which computers will be used for gateways and use a secure set of firewall rules to limit the damage as much as possible by monitoring incoming and outgoing information.
4. Create secure workstations with permissions that allow productivity offline, and conversely.

5. Set a Master Station off of the network and build in secure password protection for important files.
6. Install Linux or Unix systems for the online computers at the very least.
7. Set a security based operating system in at least 1 computer in the office and use it frequently to evaluate the security performance of your routers and monitor the tcp traffic.
8. Set up physical security protocols as in no screen shots no cellphones with cameras etc.
9. Stress test your system and make changes frequently, particularly removing old passwords etc.
10. Update the security on every machine online once per month.
11. Provide only job specific training on the machines you authorize people to use.
12. Send me a thank you card.
13. Put money in it because this next step alone could save you millions.
14. Name all of the computers something stupid and non business related and switch those names every few months.

About that last one I am quite serious. I have suggested names like Daffy's PC, or Larry123 PC, for a decade now for one reason and one reason only, "From the outside of a network that is what is visibly seen."

Picture yourself outside of a bank looking through the network on your computer and instead of seeing AC-Payable, AC-Receivable, Loans, etc you see a bunch of nonsensical names.

That theoretical bank just made it as many times harder to figure out which computer to try to hack into, as there are computers in the network.

Now over time they might find their way in to Larry 123 only now that its time to change it, they can't find that PC without starting over.

Securing Other Operating Systems

There will likely be a many of you who hold on to the idea that the main commercial systems are still preferable. Here are a few tips to make them more secure.

Up to date anti virus software coupled with a vpn and port monitoring software. Additionally do not use the home edition for business. Change the I.P. Frequently and do not store cookies of any kind on a workstation. (See Blackhole Exploit)

Windows 8, I have not evaluated but can assume these rules all stay true.

Mac, Generally Macintosh is less prone to exploits but the same rules apply due to the file sharing tendencies of the employee. Between Itunes and other such programs the potential for leaked information is far higher than with a Linux machine and that is just due to software access.

Remember you can set restrictions on what the user can do in Linux.

This will more or less wrap up this installment, I can suggest you take all of this under advisement and while there is more that could be said it remains in your best interest to get up to date and better informed about this subject by doing more research.

I can suggest that to familiarize yourself with Linux you can actually order a customized Linux distro from me if you would like to, with your company branding etc. I build them using SUSE Studio for recreation.

I would suggest you do if only to learn more about it and to show some support, so that next year I can bring you even more up to date information.

While Linux is free I would only charge you for my time and so for 40 dollars or so, you would be getting something made just for you.

Otherwise yes find free Linux distributions from all over the internet. To install one you will need a cd burner and an iso to burn onto it. Burning software if you don't have it already and its best if you get a "Live CD Distro" if its your first Linux installation.

To install from a burned cd/dvd you will want to halt your computer from booting and select the boot order so that the computer boots from cd.

We will cover full installation only for now since dual booting is a complicated affair to a new user.

When prompted select "install" and then select "Use entire disk." If it wants you to select the partition sizes remember to format to ext 3 or ext 4 for all of the partitions. Make the "Home folder" the largest, and leave room to make "memory" whatever the ram size is and the "swap" roughly the same size. (2gb max is fine for swap)

If it asks about grub say yes, if it asks about MBR it means the same thing so only one of these is necessary.

It will guide you through the installation. It will then ask you to reboot, when it does so be sure to remove the CD and when prompted start from the "Hard Disk" if the question is asked.

If it asked you more questions or wanted you to select more partitions check online to be sure of the correct sizes for your computer.

Likewise if the options are presented as they are in G Parted, you might find it confusing so check the tutorial online.

My Linux distros are generally easy enough to install even in a virtual environment so like I said before to get familiar with the process it might be worth your time to try them out.

My website is http://www.alwaysintao.com and I have a Facebook page for my Linux Distros https://www.facebook.com/pages/My-Linux-Builds/447871738637184?ref=hl

I can be reached at info@alwaysintao.com with your questions or to request a customized Linux build.

I offer no additional warranty to the GNU license because it is not a commercial product. I am not charging you for software but rather for the disk itself, the time it takes me to burn it and package it etc.

A more complex build might cost you more depending on what you want but I can offer this as a suggestion. Start by trying out something I offer for free and see what you think. (Frosty is a nice build) If you love it and want it with your company logos etc then come to me and say so.

I can send the DVD usually within the week.

Likewise if you run into a bind and need my advice you do have my email address so feel free to call upon me to consult.

(There is a fee for that but I can sometimes answer questions that save you a fortune in costs.)

Thank you for your time and I hope you found this book useful.

www.ingramcontent.com/pod-product-compliance
Lightning Source LLC
Chambersburg PA
CBHW060937050326

40689CB00013B/3127